SCIENCE BEHIND THE COLORS
MANDRILLS

by Alicia Z. Klepeis

pogo

Ideas for Parents and Teachers

Pogo Books let children practice reading informational text while introducing them to nonfiction features such as headings, labels, sidebars, maps, and diagrams, as well as a table of contents, glossary, and index.

Carefully leveled text with a strong photo match offers early fluent readers the support they need to succeed.

Before Reading

- "Walk" through the book and point out the various nonfiction features. Ask the student what purpose each feature serves.
- Look at the glossary together. Read and discuss the words.

Read the Book

- Have the child read the book independently.
- Invite him or her to list questions that arise from reading.

After Reading

- Discuss the child's questions. Talk about how he or she might find answers to those questions.
- Prompt the child to think more. Ask: Did you know about mandrills before reading this book? What more would you like to learn about them?

Pogo Books are published by Jump!
5357 Penn Avenue South
Minneapolis, MN 55419
www.jumplibrary.com

Library of Congress Cataloging-in-Publication Data

Names: Klepeis, Alicia, 1971- author.
Title: Mandrills / by Alicia Z. Klepeis.
Description: Pogo books.
Minneapolis: Jump!, Inc., [2022]
Series: Science behind the colors
Includes index. | Audience: Ages 7-10
Identifiers: LCCN 2021034070 (print)
LCCN 2021034071 (ebook)
ISBN 9781636903798 (hardcover)
ISBN 9781636903804 (paperback)
ISBN 9781636903811 (ebook)
Subjects: LCSH: Mandrill–Juvenile literature.
Mandrill–Color–Juvenile literature.
Classification: LCC QL737.P93 K54 2022 (print)
LCC QL737.P93 (ebook)
DDC 599.8/6–dc23
LC record available at https://lccn.loc.gov/2021034070
LC ebook record available at
https://lccn.loc.gov/2021034071

Editor: Eliza Leahy
Designer: Emma Bersie

Photo Credits: Eric Isselee/Shutterstock, cover, 3, 4, 23; Dean Fikar/Shutterstock, 1; Asaf Weizman/Shutterstock, 5; Nature Picture Library/Alamy, 6-7; Ger Bosma/Alamy, 8-9; Alessandro Caroli/Shutterstock, 10-11; Anup Shah/Getty, 12; Curioso.Photography/Shutterstock, 13; Thomas Marent/Minden Pictures/SuperStock, 14-15; Natalia Paklina/Shutterstock, 16-17; Edwin Butter/Shutterstock, 18; stefbennet/iStock, 19; Andrey Bocharov/Shutterstock, 20-21.

Printed in the United States of America at Corporate Graphics in North Mankato, Minnesota.

TABLE OF CONTENTS

CHAPTER 1

A FABULOUS FACE

What animal has a bright face and **rump**? This colorful **primate** is a mandrill!

Mandrills spend their days on the ground. They are **omnivores**. They look for fruit, seeds, nuts, insects, and eggs to eat. At night, they sleep in trees.

Brown fur covers most of their bodies. This acts as **camouflage**. It helps them hide from **predators** like leopards and eagles.

TAKE A LOOK!

Mandrills live in forests in Central Africa. Take a look!

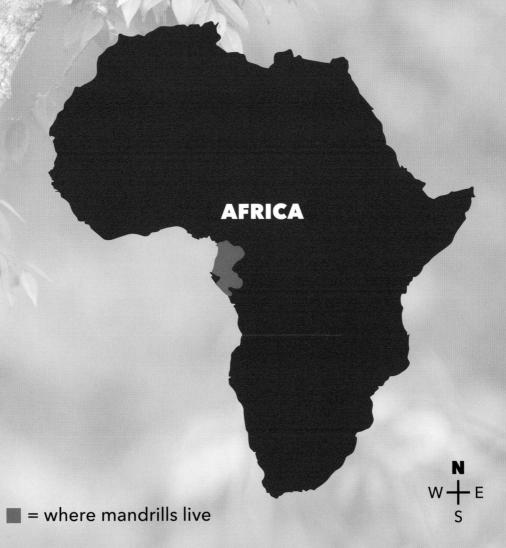

AFRICA

■ = where mandrills live

N
W ✛ E
S

Other parts of their bodies are bright. These parts stand out in forests. Mandrills have yellow beards. They have red lips. Many have red brows and noses. Blue **ridges** are on either side of their noses. Their rumps are red, blue, purple, or pink. Males are brighter than females.

male

female

TAKE A LOOK!

What are the colorful parts of a mandrill? Take a look!

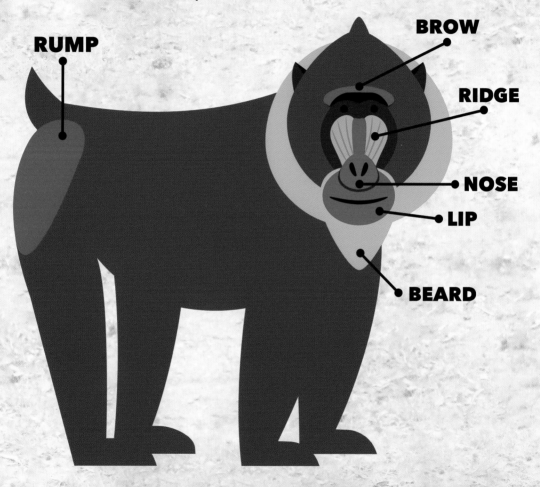

RUMP

BROW

RIDGE

NOSE

LIP

BEARD

Mandrills have many **blood vessels** near the surface of their skin. This is where the red comes from.

Light **reflects** off **collagen** in their skin. This makes the ridges look blue.

ridge

CHAPTER 2

··

LIFE IN A TROOP

Mandrills live in troops. Troops often have around 40 mandrills. Their coloring can make it easier for them to follow each other through forests.

Females choose the most colorful males as **mates**. Why? Bold colors show that a male is healthy.

Males make a **hormone** called **testosterone**. The more of this a male has, the brighter he is. The male with the brightest colors has the highest **rank** in a troop. He produces the most young.

DID YOU KNOW?

Mandrills are the biggest monkeys in the world. Males can weigh 120 pounds (54 kilograms). They are about twice the size of females.

Males fight to gain a higher rank. The winner will get brighter. Why? His testosterone level rises when he wins. The loser's color gets duller.

CHAPTER 3

LIFE IN COLOR

Mandrills are born with pink skin and brown fur. Their faces are pink. They have dark fur on their heads.

At about six years old, males start to get their bold colors. It takes several years for their full adult colors to set in.

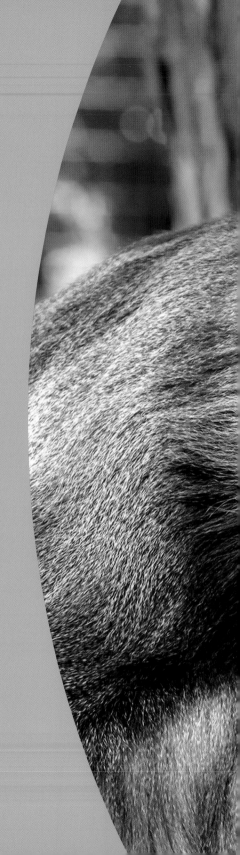

Female mandrills stay in the same troop for life. Some males leave the troop to form their own. In troops, mandrills **groom** one another. This keeps their fur and skin clean. It also helps them **bond**.

Their bright faces and rumps tell us a lot about how mandrills live. Would you like to see one?

DID YOU KNOW?

Mandrills live for about 20 years in the wild.

ACTIVITIES & TOOLS

COLOR STANDS OUT

A mandrill's bright colors stand out in its forest home. Notice how you see color from a distance with this activity!

What You Need:

- ruler
- scissors
- five different colors of fabric
- string
- clothes hanger
- pencil
- paper
- another person

1. Cut each color of fabric into a strip that is about 1 inch (2.5 centimeters) wide and 10 inches (25.5 cm) long.

2. Tie each strip to the bottom of the clothes hanger. Leave a little space between each color.

3. Use the string to tie the hanger to a tree. If you don't have a tree nearby, you can use a clothesline or a swing set.

4. Fold a sheet of paper into thirds. In the left column, write the colors of fabric in a list. At the top of the middle column, write your name. At the top of the right column, write your partner's name.

5. Standing at least 20 feet (6.1 meters) away, carry your paper and pencil and walk toward the hanger. What color do you see first? Place a 1 on the list next to that color. Number the colors in the order you see them.

6. Have your partner repeat Step 5. Do you agree on which color you saw first?

GLOSSARY

blood vessels: Tubes in the body through which blood flows.

bond: To form close connections with another.

camouflage: A disguise or natural coloring that allows animals to hide by making them look like their surroundings.

collagen: A kind of protein found in skin and tissue.

groom: To clean and take care of the appearance of oneself or another.

hormone: A chemical substance made by the body that affects the way the body grows, develops, and functions.

mates: The breeding partners of a pair of animals.

omnivores: Animals that eat both plants and meat.

predators: Animals that hunt other animals for food.

primate: A member of the group of mammals that includes monkeys, apes, and humans.

rank: A position within a group.

reflects: Throws back heat, light, or sound from a surface.

ridges: Narrow, raised strips.

rump: The rear end of a mammal.

testosterone: A hormone that occurs naturally in males.

INDEX

TO LEARN MORE

Finding more information is as easy as 1, 2, 3.

❶ Go to www.factsurfer.com

❷ Enter "mandrills" into the search box.

❸ Choose your book to see a list of websites.

FACT SURFER